Make Your Own Indoor Garden

HOW TO FILL YOUR HOME WITH LOW MAINTENANCE GREENERY

Sarah Durber

WHITE OWL

AN IMPRINT OF PEN & SWORD BOOKS LTD.
YORKSHIRE – PHILADELPHIA

First published in Great Britain in 2021 by
Pen & Sword WHITE OWL
An imprint of
Pen & Sword Books Ltd
Yorkshire – Philadelphia

Copyright © Sarah Durber, 2021

ISBN 9781526774583

Design: Paul Wilkinson
Printed and bound in India by Replika Press Pvt. Ltd.

Pen & Sword Books Limited incorporates the imprints of Atlas, Archaeology,
Aviation, Discovery, Family History, Fiction, History, Maritime, Military, Military
Classics, Politics, Select, Transport, True Crime, Air World, Frontline Publishing,
Leo Cooper, Remember When, Seaforth Publishing, The Praetorian Press,
Wharncliffe Local History, Wharncliffe Transport, Wharncliffe True Crime and
White Owl.

For a complete list of Pen & Sword titles please contact:
PEN & SWORD BOOKS LIMITED
47 Church Street, Barnsley, South Yorkshire, S70 2AS, England
E-mail: enquiries@pen-and-sword.co.uk
Website: www.pen-and-sword.co.uk

Or
PEN AND SWORD BOOKS
1950 Lawrence Rd, Havertown, PA 19083, USA
E-mail: Uspen-and-sword@casematepublishers.com
Website: www.penandswordbooks.com

Contents

CHAPTER ONE

How to Start a Plant Collection

WHEN I STARTED OUT on a quest to fill my home with greenery, I had to visit lots of different plant shops and garden centres and learn about the plants I had purchased by searching online for tips and by making mistakes along the way. I hope with this book I am able to answer some of the most commonly asked questions raised by new plant owners and help people who want to have more greenery in their lives but don't know where to start.

Once my interest in plants began, I found my own plant collection started to grow pretty quickly. It was hard to choose just one plant when I was surrounded by choice in the plant shops I visited. Even though I wanted plants to clean the air in my home, I didn't only buy these, and sometimes this was successful and sometimes this ended in tears. This book aims to help you start a plant collection that is going to last, and to help you avoid making the mistakes I made when I first started out. I've included a whole chapter on succulents and cacti later in the book, as it felt as though they needed their own section. I also think that as long as you have enough light for succulents and cacti these are a great place to start too, so you don't have to only stick to the plants I have mentioned below.

Owning and maintaining an indoor garden can be possible for anyone, and this book will give you step by step guides to creating and designing your own closed and open terrariums, air plant displays and even kokedamas (Japanese for moss ball). Included are descriptions of the equipment needed, and how to find this inexpensively so that the hobby is accessible to everyone. I am hoping that by reading this book you will discover a new-found joy of plants and nature as well as learn a brand-new skill.

Start off with a few low-maintenance plants.
Left to right: Sansevieria cylindrica, ZZ Raven and Snake Plant

For absolute beginners (or busy plant owners who want greenery with minimal input)

I'd recommend at least one of the following plants for a first-time plant owner, and also for people who don't have a lot of time for plant care. All of the plants suggested below need minimal water and can survive an element of neglect. It is a good idea to group plants in your home based on their care needs at first, so that when you come to water one, you know that the other plants in that spot in your home need watering at the same time, that way you will avoid making the over or under watering mistakes discussed in Chapter Two.

When I talk about feeding your plants, I recommend an inexpensive seaweed plant feed that you can buy online or in homeware stores. It is usually organic, although not all of the homeware stores advertise this, and is the best plant feed for your house plants. Just search online for 'seaweed plant feed' and you will find a few options.

The ZZ plant can withstand a lot of neglect.

ZZ PLANT AND ZZ RAVEN (Zamioculas zamiifolia – also known as Zanizibar Gem)

I have been a fan of ZZ Plants for a long time. They really are one of the toughest house plants going and need limited care from their owners. They have beautiful glossy leaves and with the right amount of care they will grow new shoots for you. They are actually a bulb plant, and therefore do not like to be overly watered.

Water

I would recommend watering these plants no more than once every two to three weeks, but if you were to forget to water this plant for a month then it still should survive!

Light and Temperature

ZZ Plants are a good option for lower light levels. I often use them to brighten up gloomy office spaces. They can tolerate both brighter light and being close to a window, as well as lower light levels. You will find that they should thrive in most spots in your home. You should plan to water them less often if they are in a darker position as they will be using less water and energy as they will be photosynthesising less. Wipe down the leaves regularly to remove dust particles and keep the leaves shiny. They can tolerate draughts, but they do not like to be in damp spaces.

Soil and Feeding

Repot your ZZ Plant every couple of years. They are happier in a more compact space, so only go up one pot size when you do come to repot. Make sure that the soil you use is extremely free-draining to avoid root rot. Mix in perlite with a regular house plant soil to give extra drainage. Feed this once a month in the summer.

The ZZ Raven has dark, almost black, glossy leaves.

THE RAVEN

Recently, the ZZ Raven has become extremely popular. This has dark green, almost black, glossy leaves and is very eye catching. The care is exactly the same as the regular ZZ Plant, although you may wish to wipe the leaves down on this variety more frequently, as dust shows up on the darker leaves more.

When new growth starts to appear on the plant, the new stem and leaves will be a very light, almost lime green. Don't worry, as the plant matures the leaves and stem will darken to match the colour of the rest of the plant.

VARIEGATED SNAKE PLANT (Sansevieria trifasciata also known as Mother-in-Law's Tongue)

The snake plant has got to be one of my best-selling plants. These yellow and green beauties are air-cleaning, look good and also tolerate lower and brighter light levels so are a good first-time plant option as they can go anywhere in your home.

Water

Water your snake plant no more than once a fortnight. If you over-water them you will see that the stems start to go mushy and rot, or the stems will droop. I have seen snake plants thriving in pots that are bone dry and have not been watered for long periods of time. They are definitely a fan of drier conditions. Although as a plant lover I do not really condone complete neglect of your house plants this is one of the plants in your collection that can withstand a little neglect (as is the ZZ Plant).

Variegated Snake Plant.

Light and Temperature

The snake plant can cope with lower light levels and it can survive brighter light. As with a ZZ plant, you will need to water snake plants in lower light less often than the ones getting more light. Snake plant leaves are long and flat and catch a lot of dust and particles from the air. You need to gently wipe them down once in a while to allow them to photosynthesise properly.

Soil and Feeding

They prefer a cactus compost as this is drier and more free-draining than regular house plant soil. Repot every couple of years and make sure that the roots and base of the plant are nice and compact. Feed your snake plant once a month during summer months.

AFRICAN SPEAR PLANT (Sansevieria cylindrica)

The African Spear plant is also part of the Sansevieria family. The care is exactly the same as the snake plant. These can also be placed in corners of the home with less light, and their tall tubular stems make for an interesting contrast to other leafier plants you may add to your collection. I like to include them in office installations as for a low care plant, they are slightly rarer and a great talking point. (See snake plant for care tips.)

SWISS CHEESE PLANT (Monstera deliciosa)

The Swiss Cheese Plant has been a house plant favourite since the 1970s, where its capacity to grow to ceiling height (2–3m) indoors with minimal care means it does indeed feel like a monster of a plant. In the wild they can reach heights of 20m. The large holey leaves have a jungle feel, making it also seem exotic and tropical, whilst it can live in a non-tropical environment happily. The holes in the leaves give it the nickname 'Swiss Cheese Plant'. Some early leaves grow without holes. Holes will not grow in these over time as some people think; the leaf design is

African Spear Plant.

Swiss Cheese plant
(Monstera deliciosa).

actually predetermined at the birth of each new leaf. As the plant matures more leaves will develop and these will contain the holes.

Care

To keep your Monstera happy you do not need to do much. Just avoid the plant sitting in water when you have watered it, so if possible, stand it in the shower to water it and allow excess water to leave the grower pot before you put it back into its ceramic pot.

Water

This plant can tolerate being kept relatively dry, so water once a week, and less in winter. Make sure that the soil feels dry before you water it as it does not like to be in overly wet soil. If you over-water this plant then the leaves will develop brown edges. The plant likes to be misted once or twice a week too as it is a jungle plant and therefore enjoys humidity.

Light and Temperature

The Monstera does best in filtered light or indirect sunlight. If the leaves are turning yellow or fading, then this means that the plant is getting too much light. Too little light will mean that the leaves do not grow with the signature holes in them.

You will notice that the plant will grow aerial roots; this is completely normal as the plant is a climber in the wild. These roots can be wrapped back around the plant stem or if you have one, the moss pole. I like to make sure that these get a good misting when I do mist my plant. As the leaves are so wide, they will catch a lot of dust particles so wipe these down gently when needed.

Soil and Feeding

Free-draining house plant soil is best for this plant. You will only need to repot only every few years. The plant will still grow taller even when it is in tight pot conditions. If you buy a junior plant and notice that the leaves have started to splay with growth as it matures, then you can add a moss pole to the pot and gently tie the heavy leaves to this to maintain upright growth if this is what you prefer. Feed the plant once a month in summer months.

EXPANDING YOUR PLANT COLLECTION

Once you start owning a few standalone plants in your home then you can feel as though you need more to create the ultimate indoor garden. Once the house plant bug hits you it can be hard to imagine life without indoor greenery. You should then consider creating a terrarium to add some interest to your space whilst still working with a low maintenance plant collection. The next chapters will explain what a terrarium is, and how to create your own at home.

CHAPTER TWO

What is a Terrarium?

ONE OF THE EASIEST ways to create your own indoor garden and add to your plant collection is to make a terrarium. You don't need a lot of specialist equipment, and, with a little bit of time spent getting your hands dirty, you can make what is essentially a mini indoor greenhouse. I have started the book with terrariums as they are a great way to start filling your home with plants in one of the lowest

Closed and open terrariums.

maintenance ways possible. Plus they are a fun plant project to keep you busy and to help you to relax

Before we move on to the 'how-to' part of creating a terrarium, it is worth understanding what a terrarium is, so that you can pick the right plants for yours and know how to care for it. A terrarium is an indoor garden contained in a glass jar or vessel. They are pretty to look at, self-watering (so therefore low maintenance) and easy to make.

The Background

Terrariums date back to the 1800s and were discovered by accident when a doctor, Dr Nathaniel Ward, who enjoyed botany and entomology (the study of insects) in his spare time, was working on his moth collection and put a couple of his moths into a sealed glass jar. The moths unfortunately did not survive being contained in this way, but the moss in the jar did. This led to him realising that some plants can survive in a sealed glass container, as they create their own self watering eco-system where they have everything that they need.

This discovery led to the creation of 'Ward cases', as the first terrariums were known. These were used to move tropical plants around that normally would not survive long-distance travel, and also became a great way for people to keep plants that would normally not have survived in their homes. The Victorians were able to fill their indoor spaces with greenery and they were real trend setters in creating an indoor garden.

Some of today's most popular UK house plants date back to the Victorian times and are still as hardy and as easy to care for as they were back then. For now, we will focus on terrariums and a little more about how they work.

How does a terrarium work and how do the plants survive?

There are two types of terrariums to choose from when creating one at home, and which one you want to make will determine which type of plants you use for it. One is a sealed (or closed) terrarium, and the other is an open terrarium.

Closed Terrarium

The conditions inside the sealed glass container create an eco-system which enables the plants to photosynthesise and drink water. This is the original style of terrarium.

The plants are able to survive, as when the glass container heats up
during the day the moisture inside the soil and the plant evaporate
and become water vapour. When the vapour hits the glass walls of the
container, it then condenses and causes water droplets to drip back
down into the soil so that the plant can drink.

A terrarium will need to be in a light spot, but it does not want to be
in direct sunlight as this will cause your plants inside to overheat and
die. I always suggest that facing a window is a good spot, so long as the
sun does not beam down into the glass container during the day.

The plants can breathe because the light will help them to
photosynthesise, where they will take carbon dioxide from the
atmosphere, and pump out oxygen. The carbon dioxide will come
from the soil and any decomposition taking place. Decomposition can
occur if one of the plants loses a leaf and this starts to decay. A small
of amount carbon dioxide will also be produced by the plant itself
during photosynthesis.

That is why terrariums are so popular. You can often get away with
never watering them as they water themselves. If you want to make

a closed terrarium, then you need to choose plants that like humid spaces such as ferns, Polka Dot Plant (hypoestes) and Fittonia.

Open terrarium

If you want to use cacti and succulents, or other plants that prefer drier conditions in your terrarium then you need to make an open terrarium, or a cacti and succulent garden, and I will show you how to do this in future chapters.

Left to right; Fittonia, Boston Fern (at back) and Polka Dot Plant (hypoestes).

CHAPTER THREE

How to Make a Closed Terrarium

Making a terrarium is fun and a great way to unwind.

MAKING A TERRARIUM is lots of fun and pretty easy. It's also a really good way to unwind and relax. I have hosted lots of terrarium making workshops. I am always really pleased to see people who arrive straight from work frazzled and on edge, leave the workshop appearing calmer and more content after an hour or so of getting their hands dirty and surrounding themselves with soil and plants.

What you will need

You will need some equipment, and most of the items on the list below can be found online, at your local garden centre or plant shop, or in a homeware store. Pet shops also sell some of the things suggested in their aquarium department. Quite a few of the things listed can be used for other projects suggested in this book too, so please don't feel that it is a waste to buy them. The components and tools should come in useful for your day-to-day plant care and creating more green spaces in your home.

Main components

- Pebbles for base layer.
- Activated Charcoal – if you cannot find this at a garden centre or plant shop then try your local pet store, they sell this for aquariums.
- Well-draining house plant soil misted so that it is slightly damp (but not too soggy).
- Pebbles for decoration.
- Jar or glass vessel you can close up.

Greenery

- Plants of your choice (suggestions here include Fittonia, Polka Dot Plant, ivy, ferns).
- Moss for decoration.

Tools

- Cork from a wine bottle, spiked onto a kebab stick.
- Radiator paint brush and/or make up sponge on a kebab stick to clean the inside of your jar.
- Plant mister.
- Garden sticks/long wooden kebab skewers – this will depend on how large your glass vessel is.
- Optional – long tweezers are great if you have a vessel with a narrower top.

What you can use as your terrarium

Before you get started, have a think about what you want to use as your terrarium (the glass container). I have found that Mason jars or glass cookie jars look really effective, and the opening at the top is also nice and wide, so that you can easily get your hands inside.

If you decide to go with a smaller opening at the top of your terrarium, then you may want to add a funnel to the list of equipment you may need. Alternatively, you could make a funnel from cardboard to help you get your pebbles and soil into the vessel, as well as a pair of long tweezers to help you place the plants carefully inside the jar.

This is your terrarium and your choice so have some fun shopping around or hunting down the perfect container in a charity shop or online.

Here's how to create your closed terrarium

1. Clean your jar/container. If your jar has a plastic seal, make sure you remove it so that the jar is not too airtight. Layer approximately 2.5cm of pebbles in the bottom of your jar. Give the jar a swirl to make the layer level or flat. Have fun with the colours, either using two different colours to make a stripy base layer, or by mixing up colours for a speckled effect.

2. Sprinkle a few teaspoons of activated charcoal over the pebbles.

You can make small or large terrariums.

This helps to purify the water as it moves throughout your terrarium and avoids fungus and disease spreading throughout.

3. Start to layer-in your soil. Once you have about 4cm in there, start to pat it down with the cork patter you have made. The soil will flatten into a much smaller mass. You need to keep doing this as you layer in the soil so that eventually you have a layer of approximately 10cm of tightly patted soil in your jar.

Start to create the layers of your terrarium

Use a cork at the end of a kebab stick to pat the layers down.

Remove the soil from the roots of the plant.

4. As you add pebbles, and then soil, brush any excess dust or soil off the glass and wipe down any smudges so that when it is finished you will be able to see inside and admire your plants.

5. Next, decide on which plants you want to place where. Remove the plants from their plastic grower pots (the plastic pots they come in) and gently shake and brush off the soil from the roots with your fingers. You'll need to be careful with this so as not to damage the roots

6. Using your garden stick, make a hole where you want the plant to go, and carefully lower the roots into this hole. I gently twist the roots so that it is easier to get them into the hole, but you can also just make a bigger hole if you don't want to do this. If you need to make a larger hole then you can also use the end of your radiator paint brush to help you.

Make a hole in the soil using a garden stick

Lower your plant into the hole carefully.

Pat down the soil around the plant and make sure the roots are covered.

7. Pat the soil back around the roots to ensure that they are covered. If you haven't patted the soil down tightly enough in step 3, then the hole will collapse, and it will be difficult to do. If it feels as though the soil is not firm enough, do some more patting down until it is and then start step 6 again.

8. As you add more plants make sure that you give each one space to grow and breathe. Leaving approximately 2cm between each hole should be enough. The plants that are closest to the edge of your jar should be placed about 1cm from the edge as you don't want any roots to touch the edge and singe from being exposed to the heat and light.

9. If you want to add moss to your terrarium to sit on top of the soil, then tear a clump off and then spritz the underneath and place it in sections where you want it to be. This is a great way to hide any soil and finish off your design.

10. You can add pebbles to the top to create more texture and design

Mist your moss before
you layer it into the
terrarium.

once all your plants are in. Some people
also add figurines to their terrariums. It's
now time for a final clean of your jar.

11. Spray your terrarium a few times
with the mister and close the jar. It is now
finished, unless you want to add any small
characters to it to give it more personality. I
have seen Lego figures, plastic dinosaurs and
mini garden gnomes go inside them.

Spritz inside your
terrarium before
you close the lid.

What to do next

You will now need to find the perfect spot for your terrarium. As already mentioned, your terrarium should be kept out of direct sunlight. If the sun beams down directly onto it then it will become far too hot inside the glass and the plants will die. Terrariums work well on a shelf or coffee table in a well-lit room, facing a window but avoiding direct sunlight.

For the first two weeks after you have finished making your terrarium, open it up and let it breathe for a couple of hours every few days. This helps the plants inside to adapt to their new surroundings and avoids them becoming too shocked by the new space they are in.

Troubleshooting after the first few weeks

It may take you a few moves to find the perfect spot for your terrarium, or the perfect plants for it. This experimenting is all part of the fun of owning plants and creating an indoor garden. As you get to know your terrarium and it settles into its new home, you will grow in confidence.

Don't water the terrarium, as it should have the water it needs already. If you do feel it needs some water, and that the soil and plants look very dry, then only lightly mist it, as a little goes a long way. It will be happiest with less human interaction, it has its own ecosystem, and constant fiddling with it will do it more damage than good.

If your terrarium keeps on heavily condensing over and you cannot see inside properly, then open the seal for a few hours to let the excess vapour escape. Slight condensation and misting over of the glass are a normal part of the terrarium eco-system working.

If your plants thrive inside the terrarium and grow too big for the space, then simply replant into a larger container (and be incredibly proud of yourself).

Finished terrariums.

Succulents and Cati

I NAMED MY PLANT business 'Succulence' as I love how easy it is to keep succulents and cacti alive. I loved that the word succulent invokes imagery of luscious greenery. Not all of the plants I work with or keep are succulents though, some are just low maintenance and I have suggested some of my favourite non-succulent plants to start off your collection at home in Chapter One.

You can tell whether or not a plant is a succulent by looking to see if it stores water in the plump flesh of its leaves or body. All types of cacti are succulents, yet not all succulents are cacti. To tell if you are looking at a cactus you need to look out for what is called an areole, which is the bump on the skin that the spine or the hair grows from. These spines protect the cactus in the wild from predators that may wish to eat them for their juicy, watery flesh. If a plant has areoles then it is a cactus, and not a succulent.

Some people believe that you never have to water a cactus or a succulent, but this is untrue. You do need to water them from time to time, just not very often. This makes them one of the best starter plants for beginner house plant enthusiasts and is often where house plant obsessions begin, and why I have dedicated a chapter to them. Children are especially drawn to these plants as they are often very cute. Just remember not to encourage the child into loving the plant too much and watering it too often or else it may not survive!

Succulent and Cacti care

This is a general succulent and cacti care guide. In the case of a species that requires anything different to the following, I will list the care differences when I discuss the specific plant type later on in this

Succulents are a great
starter plant.

chapter. Otherwise observing the following care guidelines should keep your succulents and cacti happy and healthy. There is also no way to list all of the succulents and cacti available to buy in just one chapter. I have focused on a few popular plants to get you started, but there are many, many more to choose from.

Water

The worst thing that you can do to a succulent is to over-water it; the plant will need watering from time to time, just not as often as most people think. Once the soil has completely dried out, give the succulent a good water. It will depend on whereabouts in your home you are keeping the plant as to how often you will need to water it, for example if it is on a south-facing windowsill getting bright sunlight all day long it will need watering more often than a succulent on a north-facing windowsill where the soil will take longer to dry out. I go with a rough guide of water once a month in the winter, and

Stand your succulents and cacti on a tray of water to water them.

once a fortnight in the summer, but get to know your plants and what they need from you by poking at the soil to check how it feels, and water on the cautious side (so less often rather than more often).

Avoid getting the leaves or body of your plant wet whilst you water it, if you have a rosette-shaped succulent such as an Echeveria and no easy way to water this, as you cannot see the soil for the leaves, then simply stand the grower pot in around 1cm of water in the sink or on a tray and leave the plant to soak up what it needs for around half an hour. I love seeing my succulents standing in the sink soaking up water; they look gorgeous and I water them all this way, regardless of shape.

Some people mist their succulents; however, I have never felt the need to do this as they are not in need of humidity, mostly being dry, desert-dwelling plants. In fact, it is actually better to ensure that they get fresh air from time to time to avoid them getting damp, so open nearby windows during the summer.

Light and Temperature

Because most succulents are native to the desert, or rocky open spaces, then they need good light levels to keep them happy. They can also withstand being on a windowsill that gets cool at night-time as this is what would happen to them in the wild. A lot of indoor plants do not like extremes of temperature and therefore do not like being on a windowsill.

When a succulent needs more water or light it stretches

As close to a window or natural, bright light as possible is the best place for a succulent. If you have placed it on a south-facing windowsill be careful that the plant does not get too scorched during summer months, however, this is rare. More common is succulents not getting enough light and being placed in a gloomy spot where they end up growing very stretched as they search for more light.

Soil and Feeding

You can buy special cactus and succulent soil from all garden centres and plant shops as well as online. This is specially produced to be extremely well draining and to help avoid root rot in your plants. If you cannot get hold of it you can mix regular house plant potting soil with sand and/or perlite mixed in at a half to half ratio. This will ensure that the soil is not too compact and does not store too much water around the roots.

Feed your plants during spring and summer only. Be careful to remove dust from the leaves using a paintbrush rather than wiping the plant.

You do not need to repot succulents very often. You can give them a few years in the pot you buy them in unless you notice that the roots are starting to grow out of the bottom of the grower pot. Only go up one pot size when you decide it is time to repot.

Remove any dead leaves as they form at the base of the plant, succulents will often lose their leaves from the bottom of the plant to encourage growth at the top.

Popular Types of Succulents

There are hundreds of different species of succulents, so I will focus only on the most popular plants within species types here so that you can easily start your collection off.

There are lots of different species of succulent to choose from.

When you look to buy new plants, especially succulents and cacti, try to avoid buying from large supermarkets and home retailers, where the plant may have been left in darkened warehouses and shop spaces without natural daylight for long periods of time.

Another thing to watch out for is any brown marks or signs of rot on the plant, as once the roots of a plant have root rot it is hard for them to recover. More often than not they cannot, and the plant will die.

If you are struggling to identify your succulent then have a look on social media sites and online search engines, as there are plenty of succulent appreciation groups available for you to send your plant image over to in order to help you find the plant name. If you buy from a plant shop or garden centre then they should be able to identify the plant for you.

ECHEVERIA

The Echeveria is a species of succulent that come in lots of colours and variations. They are recognisable by their rosette shape and are one of the most common succulent types you will find when shopping

Echeveria are rosette-shaped succulents.

Not all echeveria stay
as flat rosettes.

for house plants. To encourage
flowering, you need to give them
sufficient light; the plant will
grow a tall spindly stem with a
pink or yellow flower growing
from it during spring and
summer months

Not all Echeveria stay in a
rosette shape forever and this can
be upsetting to some customers who
buy them wanting them to stay cute and
compact. Echeveria harmsii and gibbliflora
are two types of succulents that grow rosettes
on their long stems; they can make your
collection look more interesting as they grow.

ZEBRA CACTUS (Haworthia fasciata)

Haworthia have always been a very popular succulent for my
customers. This is probably down to the stripes on the leaves, and
the fact that they offer a nice contrast to the Echeveria which is most
commonly found adorning windowsills around the UK. I have also
found that Haworthia are one of the succulents more tolerant of less
light if you have a shelf near a window that you would like to fill.

The stripes on the leaves
give it the name Zebra
Cactus.

JADE PLANT (Crassula ovata)

This is a great plant to gift to a friend or family member who is about to embark on a new business venture, as it is said to bring wealth and prosperity to the person that you have gifted it to. You often find Jade plants in restaurants and other businesses because it is deemed to be lucky, and it is also nicked named 'Money Tree'. The Crassula leaves will wrinkle slightly when they are in dire need of watering, and this plant is very hardy so can tolerate being forgotten about occasionally. They can grow to be quite large with thick stems.

Jade Plant (Crassula ovata).

ALOES

Aloes are a very popular succulent type, made especially popular by the fact that one of the types, Aloe Vera has medicinal uses too and it easy to care for at home and keep healthy. In Chapter Twelve, I will

Aloe Vera has skin soothing properties in its gel.

explain how to separate aloes and propagate them, as this succulent is one that often sprouts plantlets for you to gift to your friends.

Aloe Vera leaves contain a gel that is widely used in beauty products and cosmetics. It can be used to heal sunburn and to calm inflamed skin. It is often one of the few plants sold in health shops, and it can be found easily in greengrocers, plant shops and garden centres. Aloe Vera can tolerate being in indirect light; it does not have to be in direct sunlight like other succulents, but you should ensure that in winter you make sure that it is moved to a brighter spot.

Popular types of cactus

Whenever you handle a cactus, be as careful as possible and wear gloves if you can. I am constantly finding prickles in my fingers and becoming itchy where my arm has brushed against a Bunny Ear Cactus by accident; and the prickles can be very irritating and very sore.

A brush against a cactus can lead to very itchy skin.

Opuntia species

BUNNY EAR CACTUS (Opuntia microdasys and Opuntia rufida)

Although I have had to tweezer-out too many of the Bunny Ear cactus' prickles out of my hands for my liking, I still love these plants for their incredible shapes, which look like the ears of bunny rabbits. The smaller the plant, the cuter it is and they are extremely popular

Microdasys has yellow or white spines and rufida has reddish brown spines.

with children too, just be careful your child doesn't try to hug or stroke the plant – which has been known to happen before with tearful consequences.

I also love how as the plant matures, as the shape becomes more and more interesting and quirky. The pads of these Bunny Ear cacti look slightly shrivelled when they need a drink and as always, water your cactus only when the soil looks completely dry.

POWDER PUFF CACTUS (Mammillaria bocasana and zeilmanniana)

The Powder Puff cactus spikes have a hook at the end and can be a nightmare to get out of your skin carefully as the hook can imbed itself in your finger. The pretty pink flowers on these cacti make up for these horrid spikes though and they are a firm favourite in the cactus world. These can be found in both a shorter ball shape (boscana) as well as in a taller columnar shape (zeilmanniana).

Powder Puff Cactus.

CACTUS TRIOS

Popular due to the fact you get three-in-one plant, the cactus trio is grown using different cactus species. Here are just two examples. Golden Ball Cactus (Notocactus leninghausii) has yellow spikes on green flesh and may produce a yellow flower when it matures. This also comes as a singular plant. Column Cactus is greener with brownish spines. This also comes as a singular plant and can grow up to 90cm tall. Adding a cactus trio to your windowsill or plant collection again adds interesting shape and texture to your collection.

Left to right; Golden Ball Cactus and Column Cactus.

OTHER WAYS TO DISPLAY YOUR PLANTS

You don't just have to stand your plants in individual pots. As succulents and cacti have the same care needs, then you can plant them up into open terrariums to create an indoor desert garden. The next chapter will explain in more detail the steps to take and the equipment that you will need.

CHAPTER FIVE

How to Make an Open Terrarium

Open terrariums can come in different shapes and sizes.

IF YOU HAVE been inspired by Chapter 4 and the different types of succulents and cacti you can find to keep in your home, then making an open terrarium is an eye-catching way to display these. Unlike a closed terrarium, which needs little or no intervention as it is self-watering, an open terrarium will need watering from time to time. However, as you are using plants that prefer to be drier as they are usually found in the desert or in harsh environments, then you shouldn't need to water one too often.

As with a closed terrarium, the glass vessel you use is completely your choice. Shop around and see what you can find in charity shops and on second hand selling sites online.

Equipment you will need

The equipment needed is very similar to the closed terrarium.

Main Components

- Pebbles
- Activated charcoal
- Cactus soil (extremely free-draining) or if you cannot find this use regular free-draining house plant soil, but add lots of perlite (a volcanic material that helps the soil become airier and encourages drainage).
- Sand and decorative pebbles for the top layer
- Greenery
- Cacti and succulents of your choice

Tools

- Gloves (to avoid cactus prickles)
- Watering tray or dish
- Cork from a wine bottle spiked onto a kebab stick
- Teaspoon taped onto a garden stick
- Radiator paintbrush for cleaning the glass

Equipment for making an open terrarium.

Here's how to create your open terrarium

1. Stand your plants on the watering tray or in a dish in around 1cm of water, still in their grower pots (the plastic pot that they come in). This will give them a chance to soak up any water they need and will also help the roots to start to adapt in their new compost inside the terrarium. This is how I encourage you to water your succulents in individual pots at home too.

2. Whilst your plants are having a drink, clean your glass terrarium so that you can see inside it. Then add your first layer, which is the pebbles for the bottom drainage layer. It is better to have a good few centimetres here if you can, as you want to make sure this terrarium has lots of drainage for excess water so that the plants do not get root rot.

Stand your plants in water in preparation

3. Sprinkle 2–3 teaspoons of activated charcoal onto the pebbles. As with the closed terrarium, this helps to prevent fungus and disease spreading in the terrarium and keeps your plants healthy.

4. Next layer in your soil. If you are mixing perlite with regular house plant soil, then I would advise 1 part perlite to 2 parts house plant soil. Alternatively, you can go straight in with your cactus soil. This layer needs to be roughly the same height as the grower pots that your plants are in. Make sure that as you add layers of soil you pat them down using the cork on a stick tool you have made, so that the soil is nice and compact.

5. You now need to decide where you want each plant to go. You will need to use the spoon (or your fingers if you can fit your hands in the opening), or the cork, to create a space the same size as the grower pot of the plant you are adding to the terrarium.

6. Once you have done this, remove the plant from its grower pot and lower into the hole you have made. Please wear gloves when handling cacti as they can be extremely itchy and sore if they prick you!

Decide where you want your plants to go and make a hole.

7. Repeat this with all the plants you are using for your terrarium until you are happy with the display. Pat down the soil and mist it slightly so that it is nice and compact.

8. Next add a layer of sand to cover the soil and create a desert effect. Then add the decorative pebbles where you want them to be.

9. You can use the paintbrush to remove any soil or sand that has landed on the plants while you have been making your display.

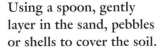

Create your hole using your hands, a spoon or your cork.

Using a spoon, gently layer in the sand, pebbles or shells to cover the soil.

Aftercare of an open terrarium.

An open terrarium can live nearer to a window than a closed terrarium as the plants you use in it prefer to get lots of light. If your terrarium is in a very bright spot it may need more water than if it is slightly away from a window – on a kitchen table for example.

To water the terrarium, you need to use a pipette or a straw to direct water to the base of the plants. You want to give the plants water every 2–3 weeks. If your mister has a narrow spout, then you can always water using this and place the end of the spout directly at the base of the plant and mist there only.

Water your terrarium at the base of each plant.

Finished terrarium.

OTHER CACTI AND SUCCULENT GARDEN IDEAS

If you cannot find the perfect glass vessel, then I have found that concrete dishes look equally striking as containers for your cacti and succulents. Concrete also soaks up excess moisture and helps to avoid the plants getting soggy. The only downside is that you do not get to experience seeing the layers you have created in the same way that you would in a glass terrarium. Follow the same steps as above, you just won't need to clean as you layer up as you will not see any streaks on the edge of the concrete bowl!

You can also plant up individual plants into smaller glass containers to give interest to your plant collection rather than just keeping your plants in a ceramic pot.

CHAPTER SIX

The Most Common Indoor Plant Problems and How to Avoid Them

THE CUSTOMERS I have met at markets and plant events, or who used to visit my shop, have often said that they have lost a cactus or equally easy-care plant in the past, and so therefore believe that they can't possibly look after any other plant as they must simply be botanically challenged. I don't believe that anybody has more skill than anyone else when it comes to plant care, it is simply a matter of knowledge and practise, and after a bit of probing, I get down to the real reason that their indoor plants didn't survive in the first place. Usually it is down to one of the following beginner plant mistakes that come up time and time again, which, in my opinion, are the main reason that most indoor plants don't live for as long as they should.

1. Too. Much. Water

This is one of the biggest indoor plant killers going. Over-watering your house plants drowns the roots and can cause root rot, unsightly brown splodges on the leaves and can kill your plant.

Make sure when you buy a plant that you check what it is called and any care tips so that you don't get home and care for it too much by giving it water every day, for example if it is a desert-living succulent. House plants generally need less water than outdoor plants as the

Don't over-water your plants, however tempting it is.

water has nowhere to go other than the pot that it is sitting in (it can't drain away into the ground as happens in the wild).

If you own a cactus, succulent, snake plant or a ZZ plant then you can over-water these by watering them too regularly. In fact, they prefer to be on the dry side, and I recommend being a bit mean with these plants and only watering once a fortnight unless we are in the middle of a heatwave.

Before watering your plant, use your finger to feel the top few inches of soil. As a general rule, if the top few inches of soil feel dry to touch then it is time to water your plant again. However, for specifics of how often you need to water your plant you should make sure you know what the plant is that you own, and then you can check for watering advice specific to that plant.

If you check with your local plant shop when you buy a plant, make sure you know what the name of the plant you are buying is, then you can follow online guides and other sources of plant knowledge (such as this book) to make sure you are not over-watering it and causing undue damage to your plant. People often think that a peaky-looking plant needs an extra drink of water, when actually it is often the last thing that the plant needs.

When you water your plant, make sure to do it over a sink or

Group plants together that like the same levels of water.

Ferns need a lot more water than other indoor plants. As well as regular misting.

bucket, so that any excess water drains out of the bottom of the grower pot. If a plant sits in water that has pooled at the bottom of its ceramic pot, then this can also cause root rot, even when the top couple of inches of soil feel dry to touch.

2. Not enough water

This is definitely a rarer issue for most plant owners than the previous one, but it can sometimes take place when a plant owner has lost a plant due to over-watering and then goes completely the other way to avoid making the same mistake. Some plants, such as ferns, require more frequent watering than others, and they also require misting and decent humidity levels. Again, finding out the name of the plant you are buying will help you to refine what care levels the plants you own need.

How often you water your plants can also be an issue when the weather changes and the sunshine begins to get stronger, or alternatively, when winter sets in and the days are shorter and light levels are lower. More often than not, your plant will let you know when it needs a drink – its leaves will droop; it will start to fade in colour, and it will look a bit sad. But before it gets to that stage, give the soil a poke to test how dry it feels – generally if the top few inches of soil feel dry then give it a water, unless your plant is a succulent and wants the soil to be totally dry before each water.

3. Choosing a plant by its looks alone.

This is a tricky issue to avoid as we all like to be surrounded by aesthetically pleasing things. When shopping for plants make sure you check beforehand by researching, or with the person you are buying from, what conditions the plant you are choosing actually needs rather than choosing a plant just based on its looks.

String of Pearls is a very cool-looking hanging succulent that needs bright light and a small amount of watering (preferably from underneath) and even then, it can be a tough plant to keep alive. However, I meet lots of people who buy it just because it looks good, for a gloomy spot or a soggy bathroom and then are upset that it didn't survive even with warnings in advance about how fussy it can be. I have always sold these with a warning that it may not survive as well as other hanging plants such as String of Hearts or Devil's Ivy, which are two of my favourite low-maintenance, hard-wearing hanging plant suggestions for most spaces. (See Chapter 7 for more details.)

Likewise, most ferns are no good for overly bright and dry spaces, as they need humidity and to have a nice level of moistness in the soil, as well as light shade. Although they look incredible, if you haven't

String of Pearls Plant looks fantastic but can be hard to keep alive.

got the time to dedicate to caring for them, or you are planning them for a dry place in the home, then my advice would be to pick something easier that requires less attention.

4. Light levels

All plants need some light to photosynthesise, but I still frequently get asked what plant would survive in a dark, window-less, soggy bathroom. The answer unfortunately is none, unless you are willing to move the plant into a naturally lit space from time to time to ensure that it gets the chance to sunbathe.

Light is imperative for a plant to survive, however, and just like with water levels, the needs of each plant will vary in terms of the light that they require; some plants prefer brighter spots, and some prefer less or partial shade. This means that you should be able to find the right plant for your space by looking at what light levels you have at home and choosing a plant based on this. It is also worth remembering that as seasons change, then light levels also change with them and you may need to rearrange your plants depending on the time of year and how much light they are getting in their respective spot in your home.

Succulents require good light levels to stay alive.

5. Too many people caring for your plants.

I once got called back to an office installation in a panic as the office manager told me that 'all of the plants are dying'. They weren't. One succulent had been overwatered and had died, but the other plants were looking parched and a bit peaky, although still alive.

After a good chat, it transpired that the plants were being watered vigorously by all of the team as they wanted to ensure that they survived. The only problem was that most of these plants only wanted to be watered once a week or less and they were being watered daily by lots of different team members! In February – when it was dark and cold, and the plants didn't need it.

The team then panicked and stopped watering them all together as no one wanted the responsibility for destroying the plants. When I arrived, the plants had been through an ordeal. We decided on one person on the team to take charge of the plant care and they are now thriving again. Make sure if you share a home or a space with other people, you decide who is in charge of the plant care so that the plants don't get too much or too little care to allow them to thrive.

Most of all, please enjoy your plant care adventure. Use it as an opportunity to learn. You may make mistakes (we all have), but you'll soon learn from them and you will often find that plants are tougher that you think. This book will give a clear guide on how to care for some of the lowest maintenance plants out there, and with a bit of time and patience you should hopefully have a thriving indoor garden at home.

Get into a routine with your plants, and make sure all people in your household know who is doing the care.

CHAPTER SEVEN

How to Create a Hanging Plant Display and Which Plants to Use for it

YOU DON'T HAVE to add lots of holes and hooks to your home to be able to own trailing house plants. Perching a plant on a fireplace, bookshelf or on a bathroom cabinet will still allow your plant to trail and fill your space with greenery without upsetting a landlord or damaging your property. Hanging plants give you the option to add greenery in hard to reach spots and there are plenty of low-maintenance options to choose from. If you are short on floorspace or have children or pets that may knock over free-standing plants, then creating a hanging plant shelf by layering in a choice of hanging plants is a good option. There are plenty of trailing plants to choose from and I have listed a few of the easiest ones to care for here to help you get started.

STRING OF HEARTS (Ceropegia woodii)

It makes sense for me to focus on the String of Hearts first as it is probably my all-time favourite plant (if I absolutely had to choose one). This is down to its extremely flexible nature: you can keep it in all sorts of spots in the home as it can tolerate humidity, so it can be positioned in the kitchen and bathroom as well as keeping it

Grouping hanging plants
on a shelf is an effective
way to display them.

in a living room or a bedroom. Caring for String of Hearts is very simple. It is a jungle succulent, so whilst it doesn't need lots of water (like a regular desert succulent) it also doesn't require lots and lots of direct light, so you have more choice of where to place it.

Care

Water

The roots on these plants are very skinny so can easily rot if you water the plant too frequently. I recommend watering them only when the soil is completely dry. You are fine to water them from the top of the plant too. In terms of frequency, it depends on where your plant is positioned as to how often you water it. For mine in my bathroom, I tend to water once a fortnight, but in my living room they need slightly more frequent watering, so once every ten days. As always, give the soil a poke to check how dry it is to determine if you need to water your plant. If you under-water them they will stop growing and you will get dry frazzled ends at the end of the stems. If you over-water them, then the leaves will turn yellow and drop off. You can easily fix your plant by giving it a 'haircut' to remove straggly stems or dead leaves and resume the correct water routine. I've often found that a trim encourages new green growth and gives the plant a fresh lease of life.

String of Hearts plant has heart-shaped leaves.

Light and Temperature

In terms of light, String of Hearts plants like to be facing a window
and receiving decent light levels, and whilst they can also survive
being placed on a windowsill in direct sunlight you will need to move
them if the light is too bright or scorching. You will know if they are
getting too much light as they get a bit straggly. Temperature-wise
they can tolerate changes of temperature without too much fuss,
which again is why I love them so much; they very rarely need you to
move their position in your home due to not liking a space.

Soil and Feeding

As they are hanging succulents, I would always use a cactus and
succulent soil for these plants. This helps the roots keep away from
root rot as the soil is so free-draining. Feed these plants once a month
in summer months. In the spring you may be lucky enough to see
delicate white flowers on your String of Hearts. You can display in
a macramé hanger or on top of a fireplace, bookshelf or bathroom
cabinet. Repot every few years.

Devil's Ivy will let you know when it needs watering as the leaves begin to droop.

DEVIL'S IVY (Epipremnum aureum)

This plant is also one I recommend for people starting a plant collection; it is great for beginners and busy plant owners. Nicknamed Devil's Ivy as it is a 'devil to kill', these plants can withstand poor care levels and bounce right back. They also clean the air of toxins so are great to have around the home.

Care

Water

Water these no more than once a week. You can keep these in humid rooms, or mist them a couple of times a week too. When these are feeling parched, you will see that the leaves start to droop, however, after watering they tend to bounce back. If the leaves go yellow you can pull them off, as this is a sign that you are over-watering your plant. Brown and crispy leaves are a sign that the plant is not getting enough water.

Light and Temperature

Devil's Ivy can survive indirect sunlight and can also survive being in slightly gloomier spots too. As long as they are facing a window then they will grow towards the light; this means that you can keep them in corners and spots in rooms where the light doesn't always reach.

Soil and Feeding

These plants are fine in regular house plant soil. You can feed them once a month between spring and autumn. You can prune these to keep them the length you need and you can try and propagate from the cuttings that you take (see Chapter 12 for more details on this).

SPIDER PLANT (Chlorophytum comosum)

Yes, Spider Plants are a throwback to the 1970s, but these plants are popular for a reason. Mainly that they are extremely easy to care for, they regularly reproduce spider babies so that you can fill your home with many more spider plants and therefore clean the air in all rooms, or you can pass on to a friend or loved one. My local online 'sell or swap' group often has people giving away Spider Plant babies and lots of people wanting to take them on.

Care

Water

I've heard people tell me they rarely water their Spider Plants, but for best practice water at least once a week in spring and summer and then slightly less often in winter. The leaves will droop when the plant needs a water, and the ends will go brown at the tips if they are getting too much light and not enough water. You can chop off any damaged or brown leaves.

Light and Temperature

Place the Spider Plant in a well-lit room away from direct sunlight. Too much light will make the leaves go brown. If you have this plant in a gloomier spot then the leaves may become faded and less green. They are also less likely to produce baby plants in gloomier spots. They are tolerant of most spaces in the home and can withstand some neglect in terms of draughts and temperature changes.

Soil and Feeding

Well-draining house plant soil is best for this plant. Feed every two weeks in summer months. Repot baby plants when you see a root at the end of the plantlet. Keep the soil moist to encourage the plant to root properly when you first move it to a new pot.

Spider Plant was a popular plant in the 1970s.

MISTLETOE CACTI (Rhipsalis baccifera)

Often mistaken for samphire by my customers, Rhipsalis is a striking trailing cactus without any spikes. In the wild it grows in rainforests and jungles. Adding this plant to any collection adds interest down to its unique texture and appearance.

Care

Water

In the wild, Rhipsalis grows in humid conditions so you can mist it every few days. Water this when the soil runs dry as you would any other cactus or succulent: around once every ten days should be about right.

Light and Temperature

As this is used to receiving light through the leaves of bigger trees, then indirect and dappled light is best for this plant. Some people think it needs to be in direct light due to the fact that it is a cactus, but

Rhipsalis is a hanging succulent with interesting texture.

this is not true. It is best to avoid scorching light levels and place it facing a window. They do not like to get too cold and avoid draughty spots.

Soil and Feeding

Rhipsalis needs cactus and succulent soil to encourage drainage. Feed it once a month in summer months and trim the leaves if they get too long. This plant is very fuss-free.

SATIN POTHOS (Scindapsus pictus)

This trailing plant is very pretty with a silvery pattern on the leaves. I often choose it as it offers an alternative shade of green when creating a plant display. It likes to trail downwards from a shelf or hanging planter. Although the pattern of the leaves gives an impression of delicacy, this plant can withstand some elements of neglect.

Satin Pothos has a silvery pattern on the leaves.

Care

Water

Water once a week. However, if you do forget to water this plant then
it will tell you as the leaves start to curl up. Give it a drink and you
should see them uncurl. This also enjoys humidity so can be placed in
a bathroom or misted regularly.

Light and Temperature

Place in filtered or indirect light and this plant will be happy. It prefers
to be warmer so does not like draughty spots or sudden drops in
temperature.

Soil and Feeding

Use a regular house plant soil for Satin Pothos, and feed it once a
month in summer months.

CHAPTER EIGHT

The Kokedama and How to Make One

Kokedama can be displayed hanging or on a surface.

THE WORD KOKEDAMA means 'moss ball' in Japanese. A Kokedama is a Japanese hanging plant display that is easy to make and it looks fantastic. If you travel to Japan you will see these hanging in lots of shops and apartments, usually grouped to create a hanging garden. Some will have extremely neat and precise string formations

around the ball, and others will be slightly more rustic looking. Because the plants are suspended in the air surrounded only by moss and string, they feel luscious and natural and give the eye more greenery to look at because of the moss.

The concept is simple, you create a ball of soil around the roots of the plant, and then wrap the soil ball in moss. You then affix the moss around the plant using string, and then you can hang the Kokedama wherever your plant needs to be (i.e. a window for plants that need light, or a shadier spot for plants who want less light)

I love using ferns in Kokedama as they are happiest with constantly moist soil, and you can ensure that this is the case by giving your Fern Kokedama a quick poke to check that your moss ball feels damp and then soaking it every few days to maintain the levels of water that the plant needs. You can also use a mister to keep the moss and the fern leaves at a good level of humidity for the plant.

How to Make a Fern Kokedama

Surprisingly you don't need very much equipment to make a Kokedama. The key thing is getting the correct soil for creating a ball shape and maintaining moisture.

What you will need

- Soil: a combination of bonsai soil and multi-purpose compost (it isn't always possible to find bonsai soil so you can try making this with a coir soil mix which retains moisture.)
- Two Bowls – one for mixing the soil together and one to catch excess water.
- Sheet Moss
- Plant of choice – the one in this chapter is a Boston fern
- Scissors
- A ball of string. (You can use waxed string if you want to avoid it changing colour over time.)

Here's how to create your Kokedama

1. Combine the bonsai soil and the multi-purpose compost in a bowl. You should use about 50/50 to create your soil mix. If you are using coir soil mix instead of bonsai soil you will need to add water to the

mix first to ensure that it has absorbed the water it needs, and then add the multi-purpose mix.

2. Add water to the bowl to create a soggy soil mixture and then start to squeeze the excess water out into a sink or second bowl. You want your soil mix to be wet, but not too wet. Think of it as a 'dough' or 'cake-mix' consistency. Create a ball of soil using your hands to shape it. Next give the ball a twist to separate it into two halves.

3. Remove your plant from the plastic grower pot and using your fingers, gently remove the excess soil from around the roots. Place the roots in between each of the soil ball halves. Make sure that all the roots are nicely tucked in. You may need to add more compost to keep your ball shape or to fill in any gaps. You don't want any roots to be poking out of the ball.

4. Next, mist the inside of your moss sheet, and start to wrap this

Make sure that the roots are covered.

Wrap the ball in moss.

around your soil ball. You may need multiple pieces or if your sheet is large enough to wrap around the whole ball, scissors will help you to create the shape you want – or you can gently tear the moss sheet into shape. You will be fixing this with string so concentrate on making sure that you encase the soil, rather than expecting it to stick perfectly around the ball.

5. Using your string, start to fix the moss in place by wrapping string around the moss ball and tying it in place. You can start at the top, underneath where the leaves come out of the ball and affix the moss in place there if you find this easiest. I usually just start to wrap anywhere as I like my string pattern to be more random. Some people like to use lots of string and create precise, neat patterns, others like to keep more moss on show. This is entirely down to personal preference, but you do need to use enough string to keep the moss secure around the ball as this will prevent soil from spilling out.

6. If you are hanging your Kokedama up, you will need to cut yourself a piece of string at the length you need to hang the plant. Attach this to any string at the base of the plant's leaves so that you hang the Kokedama from the top of the ball. If you are standing the Kokedama in a certain place in your home remember that moss is a living thing and will stay wet, so you will need a nice saucer or piece of driftwood to stand the ball on.

Ball covered in moss.

How to care for your Kokedama

Water

You will know that your Kokedama needs watering by the fact that it feels lighter to hold, or by checking how the moss feels. You should mist your moss regularly to help maintain humidity around the plant.

To water your Kokedama, you can either stand it in a dish or tray of water to allow it to soak up what it needs or you can give it a soak in a bath or a sink for half an hour. When it stops bobbing and starts sinking then you know it is heavy with water.

You will want to have something underneath it to catch any drips if you are hanging it straight back up after watering.

You can add plant feed to the bath or dish of water once a month in summer months, and you may need to increase how often you water your Kokedama when temperatures increase.

Fix the moss using string.

Light and Temperature

Ferns require indirect light or light shade so place your Kokedama in a place where the sun will not beam down on it. Maintaining humidity is key for ensuring that the leaves of your fern do not crisp up and turn brown. They will be happy in a kitchen or a bathroom.

Other plants for Kokedama

I've suggested a fern for the Kokedama as I like the fact that the moss ball helps me to keep the fern alive and thriving by staying moist. You can use other plants too and a trailing plant that works well for people who may want a Kokedama that requires less watering than a fern is English Ivy – or you could try using a Philodendron Brasil or Devil's Ivy.

As the ball of soil is usually kept pretty moist, I would avoid using succulents and cacti as they prefer to be in drier soil conditions.

Watering your Kokedama – stand in a ball or soak in a sink.

CHAPTER NINE

Air Plants and How to Display Them

AIR PLANTS ARE incredible plants to look at and a real conversation starter. Their Latin name is Tillandsias but their common name 'air plant' feels much more suited to them. The beauty of an air plant, aside from the aesthetic, is that it does not need to be planted into a pot in soil as the plants absorb water and nutrients through their leaves.

Air plants are unusual looking and do not need to be potted in soil to survive.

In the wild, their roots attach to tree branches and other plants, and they grow alongside the plants they have attached to, taking in moisture and nutrients from the atmosphere. They are not a parasite, so they do not take anything from the tree or plant they are growing alongside; they grow in harmony with the plant they are attached to.

This means that in the wild, air plants are used to good light levels, the light that they receive is dappled, as it beams down on the air plant through the branches and leaves of the plant that they are growing alongside. It is worth considering this when planning on where to keep them in your home.

They can often flower. Their flowers are usually bright colours such as pink and purple, and although the blooms do not last for very long, they are extremely striking.

Types of air plants

There are over 500 different species of air plant, but here are two of the most common ones you will find in plant shops and garden centres.

Tillandsia xerographica is a large silver air plant also known as 'Silver Queen'. It can reach up to 20cm. These air plants are striking and architectural looking and can be displayed in terrariums or on small plant stands or tripods. The mature plants will occasionally grow a purple flower when given the correct care. These can tolerate slightly brighter light levels than other air plant varieties.

Silver Queen (Tillandsia xerographica)

**Tillandia ionatha –
popular because of the
pink leaves**

Tillandsia ionatha is popular due to its pink tips. As the plant matures, the leaves become pinker. These plants will also flower, although their flowers do not last as long as the Silver Queen's. As these are smaller (around 6cm long) you can be extremely creative in how you display them.

Care

Air plants are very low-maintenance plants and require little care. As with cacti and succulents some people believe you never have to water these. This is untrue the air plant will perish if you do not give it water.

Water

It is best to use filtered water or rainwater to water air plants, as calcium in tap water can leave deposits on the air plant and block their natural capacity to absorb water and nutrients through their leaves. Ideally the water should be at room temperature so as not to cause them any damage.

You have two options of how to water your air plant. You can mist them regularly (and make sure you keep an eye out for signs of dehydration if you are only misting your plant, such as leaves shrivelling or turning brown). Or you can soak them in a sink or a bowl of water once a week for half an hour so that they take in what they need. In summer months you may need to increase how often you do this, and in winter months you should decrease, depending on how much light/ heat the plant is getting.

In summer months, you should add a small quantity of plant feed to the water. Be very cautious with this so that you do not overfeed the plant and cause the leaves to burn. You should definitely make sure that you dilute the feed down more than the label suggests for your regular house plants (try using approximately 50 per cent of the suggested amount and see how you get along).

When you have finished watering your air plants, make sure that you give them the chance to dry off before placing them back where they live. You can do this by gently shaking off any excess, and by allowing them to dry off upside down to make sure no large droplets of water are caught in the folds of the leaves.

Air plants soaking in tepid water in the sink.

Dry your air plant upside down.

To allow the plant to dry out in the light before the light goes for the day, you should water your air plants in the morning, or at least before lunchtime, so that they do not end up wet and soggy overnight, which could potentially cause them to rot.

Light and Temperature

As already mentioned, air plants are used to dappled light in the wild, so they will not suit being sat on a south-facing windowsill receiving scorching sun all day long. You can place them in rooms where they are facing the window, or on windowsills where they will not scorch.

You can have a lot of fun creating interesting air plant displays or finding quirky pieces to stand your air plants in. I have seen them displayed on pieces of drift wood, in shells, in various ceramic and glass vessels and also in terrariums.

Making air plant displays

Because air plants do not need to be planted into a pot the same way that other house plants do, they are extremely versatile. Here are a few suggestions of how to display your air plants to create interest in your home.

Air plant terrarium

One simple way to display air plants is in an open terrarium. You won't need lots of equipment for this as you will be layering the sand and pebbles and then placing your plants inside to make your display.

You'll need

- Terrarium (open)
- Pebbles (a choice of colours will make your display more interesting)
- Sand
- Decorative pebbles or shells for surface
- Radiator brush to clean glass

Make sure you choose a glass container with an opening so that your air plant gets air.

- Air plants
- Moss (optional)

1. Layer up your terrarium with a layer of sand and then a layer of pebbles
2. Clean the glass as you go
3. Place the air plants and moss inside to make your display

Aftercare

The air plant terrarium can be kept facing a window or in a well-lit room. So that it does not scorch, avoid placing the terrarium in direct sunlight.

You can mist directly into the terrarium to water it, or you can remove the air plants to give them a soak following the earlier instructions.

If you have moss inside the glass container and you mist your moss then this will create some humidity within the terrarium too.

Air plant hanging bauble

A really popular way to display air plants is in a glass bauble that can be hung facing a window. Again, you won't need lots of equipment to create this.

You'll need

- Glass bauble (to find a place to buy these simply search the internet for 'hanging glass air plant vase/ bauble')
- Pebbles (a choice of colours will make your display more interesting) and/or sand or shells
- Decorative pebbles for surface
- Radiator brush to clean glass
- Air plants
- Moss (optional)

Equipment for making an air plant bauble.

1. Clean your bauble ready to start layering in a base for the air plant. Add approximately 1cm of sand to the bottom of the bauble.
2. Next, add a layer of pebbles.
3. Add a further layer of sand and one or two decorative pebbles for the air plant to sit on if you want to create a striped effect.
4. Gently manoeuvre the air plant inside the bauble. I like to go in by placing the bottom of the plant into the glass bauble first. If I take the plant out of the bauble, I then turn it inside the bauble and remove it bottom first too. This avoids any of the leaves getting damaged or breaking when you take it out to water.

Air plant baubles are a great gift that you can make for friends and family.

Aftercare

The air plant bauble can be kept facing a window or in a well-lit room. Avoid placing the bauble in direct sunlight, so that it does not scorch.

You can mist directly into the terrarium to water it, or you can remove the air plants to give them a soak following the earlier instructions.

These make a great gift at Christmas for your loved ones.

Air plant display ideas.

CHAPTER TEN

Which Plant for Which Room?

QUITE OFTEN PEOPLE will have a specific room or spot in mind for a plant. Sometimes it will be to cover up something unsightly such as wires from an appliance or marks on a wall. Other times it is to fill a space that the eye often goes to when relaxing on the sofa or when taking a shower.

This chapter aims to help you plan plants for the two most asked after specific spaces in your home that I came across when I had my shop, as they are perhaps not as obvious to fill as say a living room. This should help you to avoid putting a plant which hates humidity and moisture into a bathroom for example, or a light-loving plant into a bedroom where the curtains are often drawn shut. It covers the most suited plants for the spaces, but of course all homes are different and will have different layouts, so this is just a guide.

The Bathroom

I have started with the bathroom as it has become one of the most popular spaces to keep house plants. Whether that is due to blogs and social media sites boasting multiple photographs of house renovations and subsequent 'bathroom goals', and those photographs featuring beautiful bathrooms with luscious plants dotted around, or if it is just down to people genuinely wanting to be surrounded by nature at all times even when bathing, I am not sure. Regardless, the bathroom is one of the most asked after spaces when it comes to people wanting to choose the right plant for the right place.

Before I go any further, I want to add here that if your bathroom does not have any windows or natural light, then you really do need to reconsider placing a plant in it. As already mentioned, all plants need some natural light in order to survive. If you really want a plant in the

space, then you will need to set a reminder for yourself to regularly take the plant out of the bathroom and place it into a lighter spot to have a 'sunbathe'. In this instance I would only suggest a ZZ Plant as it is so tough and the most likely to tolerate this level of neglect. However, I cannot guarantee it will survive as long as it should do in these conditions and you may need to eventually rehome it to a more plant-friendly space.

If, on the other hand, you have some natural light and a window in your bathroom then you suddenly have quite a bit more choice as to which plants you can place in there. It is always best to go for plants that enjoy humidity as your bathroom is likely to create a fair bit from your shower or your bath. Don't worry if your bathroom window is frosted, if anything this is a positive for plants as it means that the light coming through is filtered and ideal for their survival.

Not all plants work in a bathroom.

Trailing plants for bathrooms

I find that people often go for trailing plants, to place on top of a bathroom cabinet or a shelf in a shower. So long as they are not too high for you to reach, and you remember to water them, there is a good selection of trailing plants that will live happily in a naturally lit bathroom.

PHILODENDRON BRASIL

The green and yellow variegated heart-shaped leaves make this a very popular plant. It loves humidity and does not like to be overly watered. It is a great plant to add to a bathroom.

Care

Water

If your bathroom is pretty damp, then go for a water once every ten days to two weeks (or when the soil feels dry in the top couple of inches). If your bathroom is well ventilated, water this once a week, but again make sure that the plant is not completely saturated and does need watering.

Light and Temperature

Place in filtered or indirect light. This prefers to be warmer so avoid draughts.

Philodendron brasil.

Soil and Feeding

Use a regular house plant soil and feed once a month during the summer months. You may need to wipe off any water marks gently from the leaves if you notice them appearing in particularly damp bathrooms.

STRING OF HEARTS (Ceropegia woodii)

I have covered the care for this plant already in Chapter Seven. One of the reasons I love this plant so much is that it will suit pretty much any room in your home; as long as you face it towards a window or near to a bathroom window then it will be fine. Although it is a type of succulent it is a jungle succulent and likes to live in humidity, so even if you do not keep yours in the bathroom it will enjoy a mist from time to time.

If you do keep it in the bathroom, you may want to check how often you need to water it, based on how damp your bathroom is and how quickly the soil dries out. The roots on these plants are very fine so can be prone to root rot if the soil is too wet. I would say water about every two weeks when your String of Hearts is in the bathroom, but of course give the soil a poke to check if it feels super dry before this to make sure it doesn't need a drink any sooner.

String of Hearts.

DEVIL'S IVY

Devil's Ivy is especially good for bathrooms with little light or small
windows as it can tolerate slightly less light than the String of Hearts and
as mentioned previously is one of the toughest plants to kill. Therefore I
recommend it time and again. See chapter 7 for care instructions.

Any humidity in the bathroom won't be a problem for this plant,
and again it will simply be a case of adjusting the watering to the
dampness of the room and how quickly the plant's soil dries out
between waterings.

Generally speaking, plants in regular bathrooms do tend to need
less watering than if the same plant is placed in a drier room such as
the living room, but it is always best to use the soil test (place your
finger in the soil to feel how moist it is) before watering your plant.

Free-standing plants for bathrooms

Sometimes a small bathroom only has space for one or two plants,
either on the windowsill or next to the bath. In the case of most
bathrooms it is best to avoid succulents and cacti as they prefer dry,
desert-like conditions. Unless your bathroom is a real suntrap and

gets light all day long and is extremely well ventilated then it is best to avoid placing these in this space.

Instead there are plenty of attractive plants that will work in a bathroom and it is really down to how much space you have there as to what plants you decide on.

SWISS CHEESE PLANT (Monstera deliciosa)

The Monstera is another plant I like to place in a variety of rooms. Partly down to its gorgeous shaped leaves with the Emmental-type

Monstera next to the bath

holes in them that give it the name 'Swiss Cheese Plant' but also as it is so hardy. It is also a jungle plant so enjoys the humidity of a bathroom, and the filtered light that a bathroom gets through the frosted glass.

The only problem with a Monstera can be its size, and whilst you can buy starter plants in pots that are 14cm diameter, this plant can grow and grow and grow so it is great for bathrooms with space. If you have only a small room you may need to move it after a couple of years.

PRAYER PLANT (Maranta tricolour)

The Prayer Plant is a great choice for bathrooms as this plant needs to be misted regularly if it is in a dry room. In a bathroom this will happen automatically and means that the plant is getting what it needs every time someone takes a shower or bath. It is named the Prayer Plant as the leaves open and close with the light (they close at night-time). The pink veins on the plant are what makes the tricolour the most popular of the Maranta group.

Care

Water

The soil of the Prayer Plant needs to be at a constant level of damp, however, it does not want to be overly soggy. This means that the Prayer Plant is one that is slightly higher maintenance than some of the other plants mentioned in this book, but it is still relatively easy to care for.

Light and Temperature

The Prayer Plant does not enjoy bright direct sunlight, it prefers partial shade or to face a well-lit window so this will determine where you can place it in your home. The filtered light through a bathroom window will be ideal. As they often come in small grower pots (approximately 12cm diameter) and grow very slowly, they are also a good choice for smaller spaces. They also dislike cold draughts.

Soil and Feeding

Use a regular house plant soil. Feed once a month in summer months. They tend to grow outwards rather than upwards.

Prayer Plant leaves open
and close with the light.

Succulents on a shelf to brighten up a bedroom.

The Bedroom

If you keep plants in your bedroom then you need to ensure that you open your curtains or blinds daily to give your plants the chance to soak in some natural light. I find the bedroom is a great place to create a plant shelf display, using either trailing or smaller plants. You need to choose them based on how much light your room receives. Succulents are a great choice for smaller spaces, but please only add succulents if your space is bright and receives good light throughout the day, and choose succulents such as Jade Plant, Haworthia and aloes that can withstand slightly lower light levels compared with other succulent varieties. (See Chapter Four for more succulent care.)

SNAKE PLANT

One common worry that I have heard from people is that they shouldn't have plants in the bedroom as they will affect the air quality of the room whilst they are sleeping. I disagree with this thought process and I would always suggest having a Snake Plant by your bedside simply because these plants pump out oxygen at night time; I have quite a few in my bedroom. They can survive lower light levels too, and therefore are good for bedrooms with less light.

Snake Plants give out oxygen at night time.

Hanging Plant Shelf

Another great way to have plants in your bedroom is to create a bespoke hanging plant shelf using the plants discussed in Chapter Seven. Most of these plants: Devil's Ivy, Satin Pothos and Spider Plant can survive with lower light levels so will be fine if you leave your curtains drawn every once in a while.

CHAPTER ELEVEN

How to Propagate Your Plants

ONCE YOU HAVE started a plant collection, and kept your plants alive with success, you may find that your thoughts move on to propagating plants and sharing your plants with your friends and loved ones. This chapter will explore some popular techniques and explain how to go about them.

THE CHINESE MONEY PLANT (Pilea peperomioides)

Chinese Money Plant has many nicknames. It is also known as Pancake Plant (due to its circular, flat leaves), UFO Plant (same reason), Missionary Plant (due to the fact that a Norwegian missionary named Agnar Espegren brought it back to Europe with him from China in 1946), and my personal favourite: Friendship Plant.

When these plants reached Norway in 1946, they soon spread throughout Scandinavia due to amateur indoor gardeners growing their own from cuttings and then sharing the cuttings. It was only in the 1980s that they became correctly named following an article in Kew Magazine. Before that they had not always been identified as Pilea peperomioides.

Chinese Money Plants have become much sought after over the past few years; they are not always the easiest to get hold of as they are relatively slow growing, so can be costly to buy outright, since commercial growers take a while to produce them.

They are still more often shared between plant owners due to the ease in which you can propagate them, and this chapter will go into more detail about that shortly.

**Chinese Money Plant
has pancake-shaped
flat leaves.**

Care

In terms of care, the Chinese Money Plant is a very low-maintenance house plant and with the right treatment, will hopefully produce you lots of 'baby' (or pups) plantlets that you can propagate and share amongst your friends and family.

Water

To care for the Chinese Money Plant, water it approximately once a week. They do not like to completely dry out between each watering, so do the finger test to check that just the top couple of inches of soil has dried out. At the same time they dislike overly soggy soil or sitting in water so ensure that you water these over the sink to allow the excess water to drain. Give the plant a mist every few days as it enjoys humidity, and wipe the large flat leaves gently when they start to gather too much dust.

Light and Temperature

This plant likes a good amount of light and a constant temperature, so avoid very cold spots, spots too close to a radiator or draughty spots. Position the plant so that it is facing a window or close to natural light, but without direct sunlight hitting the plant itself.

Soil and Feeding

When propagating, use a high-draining house plant soil or mix your regular potting soil with perlite to encourage drainage. Feed this plant in spring and summer months once per month.

How to propagate a Chinese Money Plant

It is a very special feeling when you see a 'baby' plant (pup/plantlet) growing off your Chinese Money Plant for the first time. Most plant owners want to propagate this properly without causing any damage to the mama plant, and so that they can pass on a new plant to one of their friends (hence the name Friendship Plant).

1. Wait until your pup has grown to around 3 or 4 inches high. This will give it the greatest chance of survival. You should also wait until spring as this is the best time to repot or propagate any house plant.

2. Gently remove the soil from the plant so that you can see as much

Mama plant with 'pups'
growing from it.

of the root system as possible and you can see where to make your cut. You will need super sharp snippers or a knife for this.

3. Next remove the pup from the mama plant by slicing it away from the main plant. Gently untangle any roots that are intertwined between the pup and the main plant so that you have a completely separate plant. Repeat this until you have all of your plants separated.

4. Repot all of your plants into new grower pots. Don't choose grower pots that are too wide for the baby plants. I recommend around 6cm diameter pots for your pups, and then check if your mama plant needs to go up a pot size or not, based on how root bound it was when you removed it from the original pot. Root bound is when the roots are growing outside of the grower pot through the holes, and where the roots are twisted around on themselves a lot and look as though they need more room.

Remove the excess soil from the roots and gently untangle them.

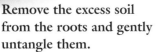

Repot the pups into smaller pots.

5. If any of your pups do not have good root systems, then you may wish to place these into water in a glass jar to encourage root growth before you plant them directly in soil. To do this, fill a glass container with water and lower in the plant. Place on a windowsill and change your water every week to keep it fresh and clean. Once you have seen roots on the plant and they have been developing for 4–6 weeks, move on to step 4.

6. To ensure successful growth of the plantlets, keep a keen eye on your soil. Make sure that this is lightly moist (not too soggy) but does not dry out completely. Mist the plants regularly, and keep in a spot with good light levels, but without direct sun hitting the plants.

   Pass them on to your friends and loved ones and encourage them to do the same when their plants gift them with pups themselves!

Money Plant in water propagation system.

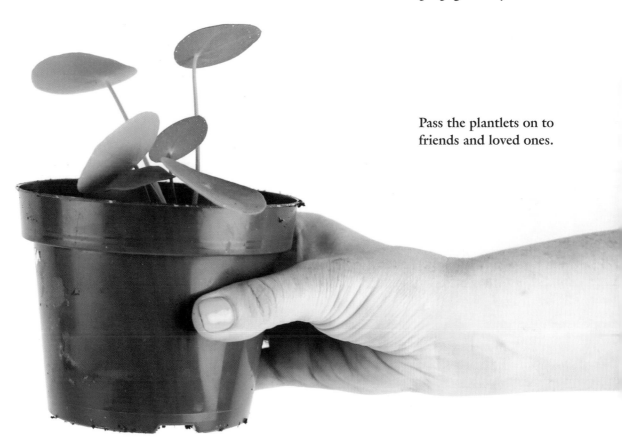

Pass the plantlets on to friends and loved ones.

Other plant propagation techniques

It isn't just the Chinese Money Plant which is easy to propagate and take cuttings from. There are plenty of low-maintenance plants that are equally as easy to propagate and share with your friends. Here are a few more techniques you can use to grow your plant collection at home without needing to go out and buy more plants. Remember this will take some practise and not all cuttings will root and not all rooted cuttings will survive when you plant them into their pots, but it is worth the time and patience getting it right to grow new plants from your current collection.

Splitting plants

Aloe Vera is an easy-care succulent that has multiple benefits. It cleans the air in your home, keeping you healthy and it also contains a sap which has skin-soothing properties when applied to sunburn or rashes and other skin disorders, so it makes sense that this is a good plant to share amongst your friends and family. (See Chapter Four for care tips for Aloe Vera to keep it thriving.)

Aloe Vera with pup.

Following the same technique as for the Chinese Money Plant, you can separate any baby plants from the main plant and repot these to now be their own plant. You will often find that aloes grow in multiples and can be separated out as they get larger and repotted so that you can spread them out around your home or gift to friends. This will also create more space for the plant and encourage further growth.

I find that it is best to plant these directly into cacti and succulent house plant soil rather than use the water propagation technique as succulents prefer not to get their roots too wet, although some people find that the water technique works well for them.

Sansevieria also grow new plantlets alongside their mama plant which can be gently separated from the main plant. You should find that these come apart more easily than aloes or Chinese Money Plants by gently using your fingers to remove the soil and separate from the main plant.

The Water Propagation Technique

A popular technique for propagating is to take a cutting from a plant, place it in fresh clean water in a glass vessel and stand it on a windowsill to encourage roots to grow. You don't need to use any specialist equipment for this at all, but you can use decorative jars or vases to make interesting displays in your home while the roots are growing.

Sansevieria also produce plantlets.

Choose decorative glass vessels to create a nice display when propagating cuttings.

1. If you are going to be taking a cutting from a plant, make sure you cut this from just below the node. This means finding the bump or nobble on the stem where there has been a leaf joint. Then cut or snip this straight across using a very sharp knife or snippers. Aim for your cutting to be between 3 and 6 inches long.

2. Place the cutting in a clean fresh glass container and stand it on a windowsill. Refresh your water every week. Wait for the roots to form and keep them growing for 4–6 weeks before potting the plants in soil.

Succulent Propagation

It can be sad to see a succulent lose its leaves at any point, but if you have a few succulent leaves at home that you are unsure what to do with you can try and grow new plants from these. Or you can gently remove some of the leaves from the main plant if you are keen to propagate this one.

1. You need to make sure your leaf has had a nice clean break from the plant stem. Then leave it for 2–3 days to scab over and start to dry out.

2. Next, place the leaves onto soil covered with pebbles. You can water the soil regularly so that it does not dry out. Try to avoid soaking the leaves – using a mister makes this easier.

3. You will see roots start to form and grow towards the soil and small succulent rosettes start to form. Once you have had roots for a couple of weeks, plant them directly into the soil and keep the soil watered regularly to avoid the roots completely drying out.

4. The succulent will grow very, very slowly. Don't worry if not all your cuttings make it to roots stage or form small rosettes. This is completely normal and with practise you will start to learn which place in your home is best for encouraging these to grow.

Place your succulent leaves on a tray of pebbles over soil and keep the soil damp.

CHAPTER TWELVE

Plants and Well-being

IT IS VERY popular at the moment to read about the latest wellness trends and fads, and how to make yourself happier or calmer using various methods. This chapter explores how plants can help improve your mental well-being and why. When I was working long unhappy hours in a grey and dull office on an industrial estate, which took me over an hour to commute to, I started to surround myself with plants at home.

It was a combination of both being inspired by photographs of immaculate Zen-like interiors on Pinterest and Instagram, all of which were finished off by a beautiful lush green plant, and the need to escape my city life and to be surrounded by nature. I just felt so much better when I had greenery around me.

Biophilia

'It's been proven by quite a few studies that plants are good for our psychological development...we need them in some deep psychological sense, which I don't suppose anybody really understands yet.'

Dame Jane Morris Goodall primatologist and anthropologist

The innate human need to be around nature is called 'Biophilia', and it makes perfect sense to me. It was introduced by Edward O. Wilson in his 1984 book, Biophilia. There are now architects who work only in Biophilic design, creating spaces that help the people in them reconnect with nature, as well as feel calmer and less stressed.

If you have ever felt immediately better by stepping outside and breathing in fresh air, away from tall imposing buildings, busy traffic

and air pollution, and then craved the same feeling at times when you have been busy at work and rushing around and feeling 'stuck' indoors, then you will also understand this desire to be near the natural world and plants that can strike at any time.

I feel happiest when surrounded by greenery.

How else can plants help with well-being?

When I started my home plant collection, I had one focus: plants that cleaned the air. I was convinced that my window-less seat in my stuffy office was the cause of me constantly catching colds, bugs and anything else that was going around. I wanted my home air to feel fresh and airy, and I was freaked out by the idea that in the area that I lived in had some of the most polluted air in Europe.

I'll go into more detail in Chapter 13 about air-cleaning plants. What I discovered by starting my indoor plant collection though, was that plants that didn't necessarily 'do' anything, other than look pretty, also made their way into my shopping basket. I left the house that morning planning on picking up a couple of big air-purifying plants and came home with a whole load more than that, as I was tempted by adorable-looking succulents and cool-looking cacti in pretty plant pots.

Succulents and cacti make me smile.

I now had plants that looked good, and needed minimal care from me, however, they still needed some care. I discovered that getting to know my plants, and what they needed from me was a great feeling. A watering session and a leaf-shining session can really boost your mood. When you have a few plants in your home, a watering and plant care session can be an event. This is a time when your focus is

Aloe and Haworthia.

on the one task, checking in on your plants, noticing any changes in them, and making sure they get what they need from you. It is extremely easy to zone out from anything else other than this task, which is a wonder in itself, calming your mind from a pressing 'to-do' list and any worries or racing thoughts you may be having at that time.

My job at the time involved a lot of travel, and I was the chief plant carer at home. Because I had done my research, and on the whole chosen plants that did not need regular watering and could survive a little neglect, they survived when I had to go away for a couple of weeks at a time. I would come home, give them a water and check them. Keeping my plants alive and learning what they liked and disliked was extremely satisfying, which in turn meant that I felt a boost in self-esteem and confidence in a new-found hobby.

I also naturally veer towards spaces that are filled with healthy looking plants. I filled my local yoga studio with greenery through the plant installation side of my business, as well as many cafes, restaurants and offices. I have often chosen to give my custom to coffeeshops, eateries and even my hairdresser, based on how much greenery they have inside their premises.

Watering your plants is calming.

Studies have proven that being around plants has lots of positive effects on mental well-being, such as improved concentration, reduction in anxiety and depression and better memory function.

Plants can also reduce pollution and I've always felt better breathing in fresh air. A trip out of the city into the countryside can solve so many worries, or at least give you a fresh perspective on them without the noise and the distractions of the city itself. It isn't always possible to escape though and that's why I wanted my home to be filled with plants, so that I had nature around me when I couldn't make it to nature itself. Hopefully this book will have helped to inspire you to fill your home with plants and improve your mental well-being too.

There are plants of all shapes and sizes to choose from.

Caring for your plants
is a great way to zone
out for a while.

Plants and plastic

The one part of working with plants that I haven't enjoyed, is how much plastic waste there is involved with the plant industry. There are a few simple ways you can help to reduce this yourself and you can encourage your local plant shop or garden centre to help too.

All the plants that are grown in Holland are shipped over on large plastic trays. My suppliers allow me to send these back to them, and they in turn send them back to Holland to be reused. It isn't ideal, but it is a small step in reducing single-use plastic, and until the industry comes up with a way to transport the plants without using plastic trays, it is better than nothing.

Plants also usually come in plastic grower pots. There are some suppliers making steps to use coir pots (post made from the fibre from coconut husks), which are great, so you can try and buy plants in these pots when you see them. You can also ask your local plant shop or garden centre for spare grower pots, or arrange a swap of these yourselves. That way when you come to repot a plant, you can reuse a grower pot rather than heading out to buy one. My shop used to have a basket of these outside for people to take for free, and again this was just one small step in reducing plastic waste. I often walk past skips with grower pots in them and I take them out to reuse or give to customers; see if your local plant shop has a similar initiative.

Likewise, try and propagate your plants following the steps in Chapter Eleven and gift them to friends to encourage them to own more greenery, and discourage buying of new plants. Aim to choose low-maintenance plants that are suitable for your space, so that you have fewer plant casualties, and again less wastage.

Reuse plastic grower pots
where you can.

CHAPTER THIRTEEN

How to Combat Air Pollution Using Plants in Your Home

I'VE MENTIONED ALREADY that my plant collection started because I was on the lookout for air-cleaning plants. I just happened to get distracted by cute succulents and cacti and start on a journey of making my home greener using lots of other plants too. I still always fall back on these plants when making suggestions for people wanting greenery in their own homes as I love the fact that there are extremely low maintenance and beautiful plants available that are useful too.

NASA published a study back in 1989, which listed plants that were best for removing chemicals from the air, as they had researched into which house plants were best to have in space stations. They focused on plants that removed toxins such as benzene, formaldehyde and trichloroethylene from the air. This was in order to reduce 'sick building syndrome'. All of the chemicals they were looking to reduce in the atmosphere are found in everyday items such as paint, shampoo, cleaning products and even cushions, and are also known as VOCS (volatile organic compounds).

I use lots of these plants from this study in my office installations for workspaces, and I focus on the ones which are the easiest to maintain. Further plants made it onto the list, but the ones I am featuring in this chapter are the ones best suited for beginners.

As a side note, to really feel the effects of plants in the home you do need to have a large volume of plants in your space (one per 20

Air-cleaning plants
are a great addition
to any home.

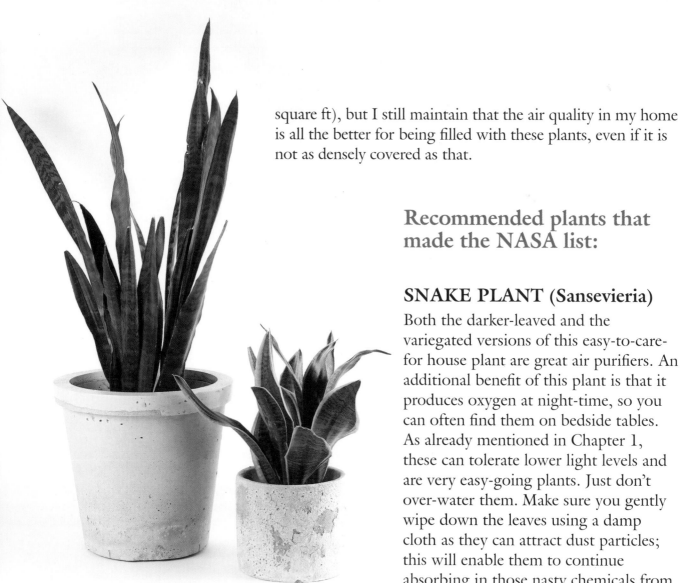

square ft), but I still maintain that the air quality in my home is all the better for being filled with these plants, even if it is not as densely covered as that.

Recommended plants that made the NASA list:

SNAKE PLANT (Sansevieria)

Both the darker-leaved and the variegated versions of this easy-to-care-for house plant are great air purifiers. An additional benefit of this plant is that it produces oxygen at night-time, so you can often find them on bedside tables. As already mentioned in Chapter 1, these can tolerate lower light levels and are very easy-going plants. Just don't over-water them. Make sure you gently wipe down the leaves using a damp cloth as they can attract dust particles; this will enable them to continue absorbing in those nasty chemicals from the atmosphere.

RUBBER PLANT (Ficus elastica also known as India Rubber Plant)

The Rubber Plant is available with dark glossy leaves or there is also a variegated version with yellow leaves. Some variegated varieties known as 'red' contain tinges of pink too. When new leaves are sprouting, they arrive in a lovely pink bud which then drops off when the leaf has appeared.

Care

Water

Rubber Plants need watering once a week or when the top few inches of soil have dried out. They can tolerate being drier rather than having sodden soil. Mist occasionally.

Dark Rubber Plant and Variegated Rubber Plant leaves.

Variegated Rubber Plant

Light and Temperature

The plants prefer indirect light and partial shade. The plants with colourful leaves need slightly better light levels than the ones with dark glossy leaves. They do not like to be placed in draughty spots in the home and prefer a constant temperature rather than extreme dips. Wipe down leaves once a month.

Soil and Feeding

They need a well-draining house plant soil. Feed the plant every two weeks from spring to summer and you will find you need to add a couple of inches of top soil to the plant each year. Repot when your plant becomes pot bound or when the plant becomes too tall for its current pot.

PARLOUR PALM (Chamaedorea elgans)

I love these palms because they make any space feel tropical and 'jungly'. They also come in a nice variety of sizes and are relatively easy to care for.

Care

Water

Parlour Palms need to be watered around once per week in summer, less in winter. Check the top 3 inches of soil is dry before watering. They like humidity too so you can mist these regularly. Wipe the leaves gently

Parlour Palm.

with a damp cloth. Commercial leaf shine products are too strong for palms and can damage them so only use water for cleaning them.

Light and Temperature

Whilst they do not want to be in direct sunlight, they do need decent levels of light so prefer to be in well-lit rooms away from any direct beams of light. They do not like to get too hot in summer. If you notice that the ends of the leaves are going brown this may indicate they are getting too much light and heat.

Soil and Feeding

They prefer soil-based mixed with multi-purpose compost. Only repot these in spring. Feed every two weeks in summer months. The bottom fronds will brown off and die as the plant ages and you can prune these off to make the plant look more attractive. This is completely normal and so long as the upper part of the plant is luscious and green you have nothing to worry about.

SPIDER PLANT (Chlorophytum comosum)

Not only can you breed these very easily at home and care for them without much effort (see Chapter 7 for full care instructions), but Spider Plants have the added benefit that they remove toxins from the air. This makes them even more of a plant bargain in my eyes, you get a lot of benefits from this one simple, easy-to-care-for plant. They are often pretty inexpensive to pick up too.

DEVIL'S IVY (Pothos Plant)

Just like the Snake Plant, this plant is one I have mentioned in many chapters due to its versatility and un-killable nature. It has a special place in my heart and that is also down to its air-cleaning properties. You can place it in most rooms in your home and it will thrive. It tells you when it is thirsty and forgives you when you give it a drink by bouncing right back. For full care instructions see Chapter Seven.

Spider Plant and
Devil's Ivy.

PEACE LILY (Spathiphyllum)

The Peace Lily is slightly higher maintenance than the other plants on this list, but I include it as with the right care it is a rewarding plant to have at home due to its beautiful flowers and glossy leaves. It also tells you when it is lacking water as the leaves start to droop, so it gives you every chance possible to keep it happy.

Care

Water

The roots of the Peace Lily like to be moist and humid. To achieve this, you can stand the grower pot on top of pebbles that are topped up with water. You will need to ensure that you keep an eye on the soil to make sure it does not dry out, so this plant may need watering more often than others in this book. Adjust watering based on how the soil moistness changes in winter. As the Peace Lily likes humidity, bathrooms and kitchens are a good spot for this plant.

Peace Lily.

Light and Temperature

Avoid strong sunlight as that will damage the plant. A room that is well-lit but not in direct sunlight is best. In the winter, ensure that the plant is getting enough light. Peace Lilies like to be warm so avoid draughty spots for this plant.

Soil and feeding

House plant compost is good for this plant. Feed every two weeks in spring and summer months. When the flowers have died, simply snip the stems off as close to the base of the plant as possible. In the right conditions your plant will rebloom. Repot once a year in spring.